EVERYBODY HAD A YUCKY TIME

How to explain 2020 to kids (in rhyme)

Science and Facts Edition

Christopher Buttons

This is a reversible book! Flip it over for another edition.

ISBN: 978-0-9982197-9-0

HOLY MOLY!

Bad things have happened aplenty - much of it in 2020.

In fact,
the whole year has been kind of rough,
jam-packed with truly yucky stuff!

What kind of yucky stuff, you inquire?
This book tells of many things dire.

Be warned, they are
REALLY frightful.

If you're scared, we
can do something
more delightful.

But if there's bravery within you, then let's dare continue.

The first yucky thing to transpire:
koalas' homes destroyed by fire.

But why did this
happen, you might ask?

Stopping climate change is a daunting task.

If people stopped making the planet warm, there'd be fewer fires and no cause for alarm.

Yucky meter

The next yucky thing was a terrible
sickness that spread.
Many ended up in a hospital bed.

The sickness expanded far and wide.
Soon the whole world needed to stay
inside!

The sickness made people scared,
our leaders were not prepared.
They waited too long to act,
and recklessly downplayed the impact.

With the
sickness
out of
control,
it took
quite a
toll.

No more movies, sports, vacations, or playing with friends at school. This sickness was downright cruel!

Yucky meter

With the spread of the
sickness growing stronger,
some workers and jobs were
safe no longer.

To do their part,
they worked in isolation.
Some, laid off, lost their
homes in devastation.

Losing your home is a yucky thing.
What more can 2020 bring?

Surely the
bad news
is coming
to an end.

An officer's job is to keep the peace,
except when bad people are police.
And some who were evil to the bone,
mistreated others with a different skin
tone.

The people didn't think it fair, so they marched in anger and despair.

Yucky meter

Portland

Minneapolis

Our leaders failed to make us united,
instead their actions only incited.
Protests endured night and day.
Did curfews stop them? No way!

Louisville

Breonna Taylor

SAY HER NAME

If those in power
stay in charge,
these protests will
remain quite large.

Yucky meter

The next yucky thing drew our gaze;
the whole sky turned orange in a
smoky haze!

How can that be, you'd pose the query?
Well, climate change isn't just a theory.

Not to be outdone by fire running amok,
hurricane after hurricane fiercely struck.

Towns flooded and
buildings fell,
it's a sad story where
we won't dwell.

Yucky meter

Okay, okay, let's take a break.
Reading about yuckiness is a mistake!

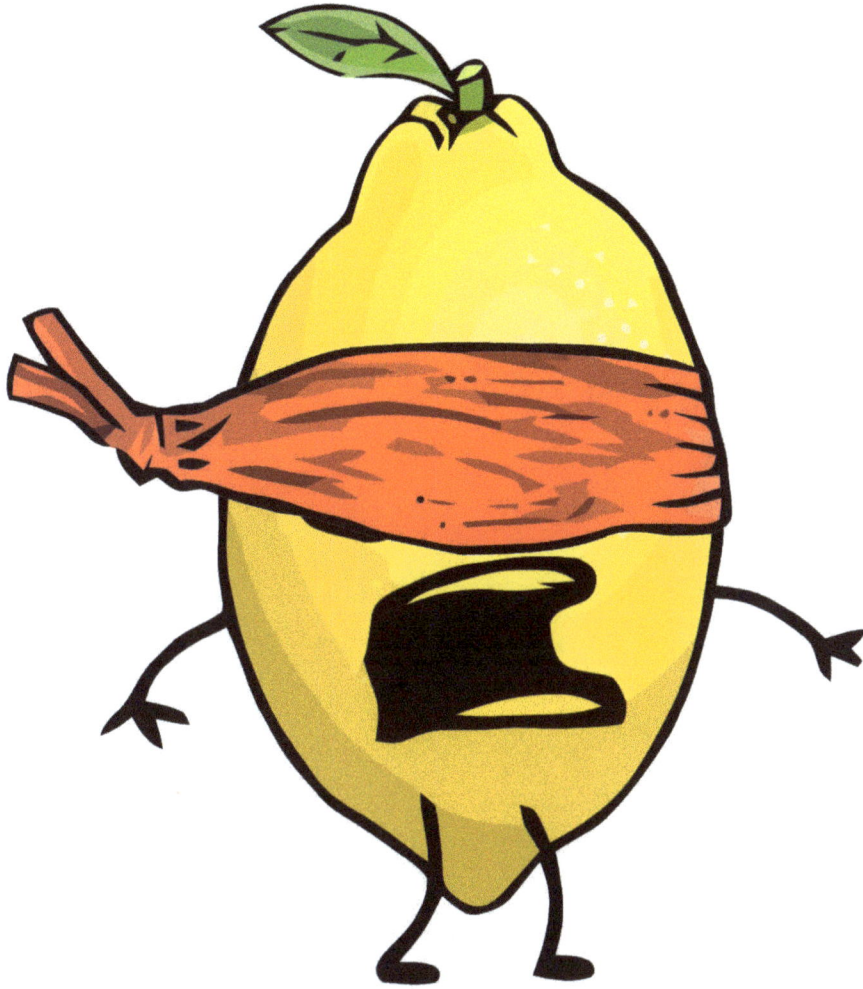

When you're ready to engage,
let's turn the page....

Yucky meter

The next thing that happened filled
us all with dismay;
an important decision maker
passed away.
She was a hero in many ways.
Our road to recovery will be a maze.

Without her leading,
the future is iffy.
Her replacement arrived
in an untimely jiffy.

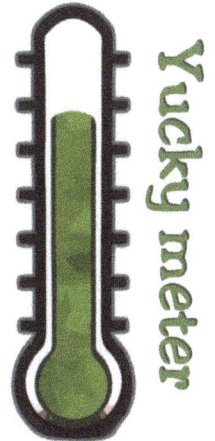

Yucky meter

At last our leader would be replaced,
our battered nation amply defaced.

Even though his time did expire,
the president refused to retire.

Too stubborn to concede,
it was embarrassing, indeed.

Yucky meter

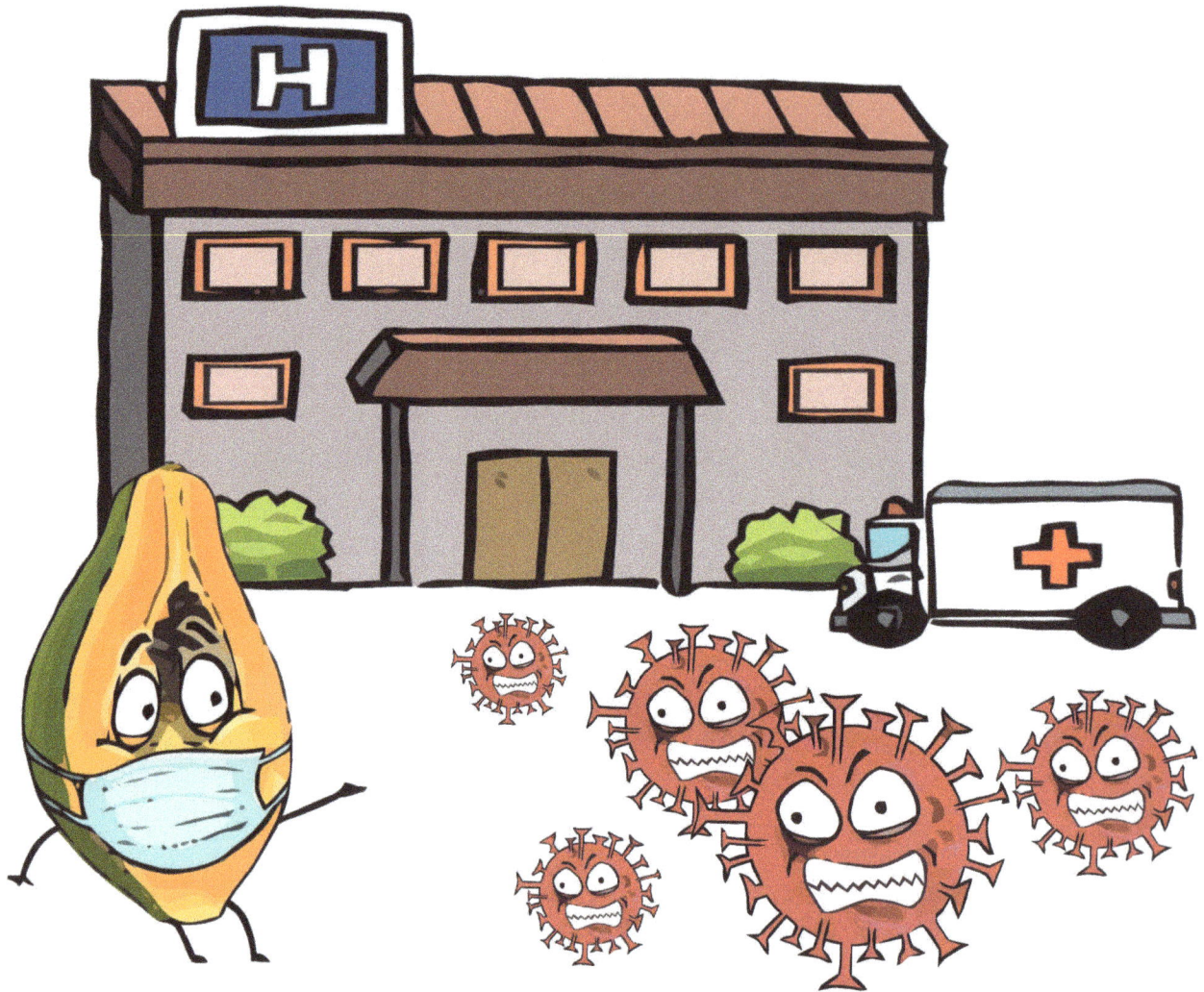

We should circle back, it's worth a mention -
that sickness from earlier gained more attention.

Oh, you thought that went away?
No, no. It's here to stay.
Record numbers were infected,
far greater than anyone expected.

UH OH!

Yucky meter

Our yucky meter's reached the top!
Will the chaos never stop?!

Good riddance to this yucky year!
May better times ahead be near!

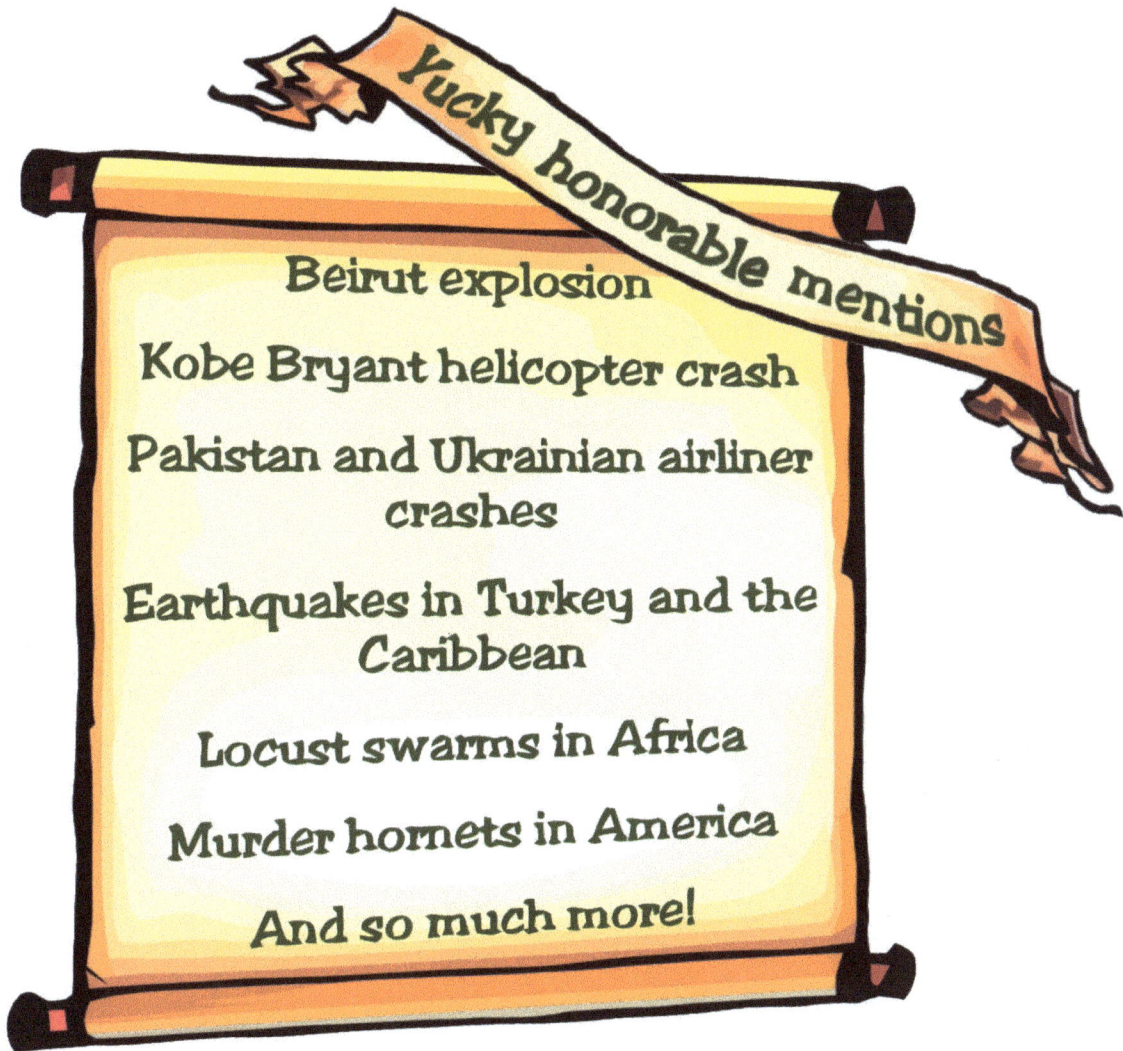

Yucky honorable mentions

Beirut explosion

Kobe Bryant helicopter crash

Pakistan and Ukrainian airliner crashes

Earthquakes in Turkey and the Caribbean

Locust swarms in Africa

Murder hornets in America

And so much more!

We can't end on a note so bleak!
Things that broke the yucky streak:

People came
together to
rebuild
stores.

Food drive
volunteers
came out in
scores.

Strangers who learned to sew, made masks for those they did not know.

Pollution declined, benefiting mankind.

So no need to mope, there's reason for hope!

Flip me over

USA! USA!

Our president may be gone, but our M.A.G.A. ways will carry on!

Flip me over

The book can't end just like that!
The last page had yuck on our hat!

Let's be more...
unrealistic
(like our
president's best
characteristic):

We're rounding
the corner,
everything's okay!
The economy's
booming, vaccines
coming any day!

Could it get any yuckier?!
Surely next year will be luckier.

Yucky honorable mentions

Almost starting a war with Iran

Defunding the WHO during a global pandemic

Suggesting injecting bleach could be good!

Discouraging testing as it makes our numbers look bad

Casting doubt on mail-in ballots

And so much more!

Look at all this yuck, splattered.
Our M.A.G.A. ways, shattered.

Oh, you thought that was done?
No, no. It's just begun.
Our wise leader let the states
do their own thing.
*What use could a national
strategy bring?*

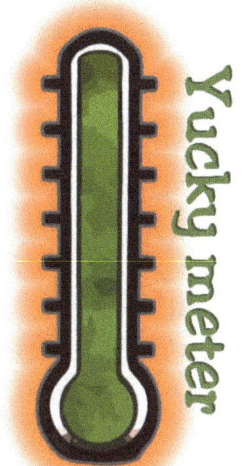

UH OH!

Yucky meter

Meanwhile, that sickness from earlier grew in audacity.
Hospitals were struggling, nearing capacity.

It was simply time for it to end.

Farewell, our M.A.G.A. friend.

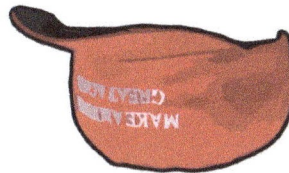

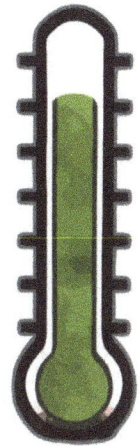

Apparently
our great
leader shined
too bright.
He gave us
overwhelming
might.

The nation
couldn't
handle
magnificence
so radiant,

despite seeing him every day in
orange gradient.

Our president hurried to find a
replacement that would last.
*After all, election day was
approaching fast.*

Soon enough there
were respects to pay,
an important decision
maker passed away.

Yuckiness this extreme could give you a bad dream.

But if you really need, we can proceed.

Yucky meter

Hold up, M.A.G.A. crew!
Let's not bite off more than we can chew.

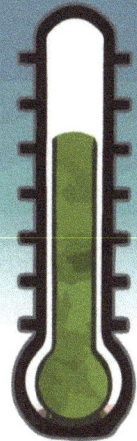

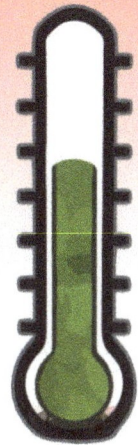

The next yucky thing that took place was a series of fires that burned at record pace.

You're not going to believe this, it's pretty crazy.
The sky turned orange and very hazy!

Louisville

Breonna Taylor

SAY HER NAME

"Subdue the thugs" was our
great president's stance
(he thought that might give
his reelection a chance).

Yucky meter

More protests lasted a very long time,
some causing an increase in crime.
More police botched their jobs,
drawing the ire of angry mobs.

There were protests and smoke,
store windows that broke.
Chaos befell the streets,
despite the president's
super helpful tweets.

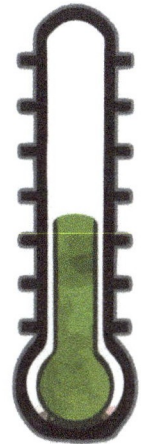

Yucky meter

Black lives matter? *So do ours!*
Sure as our flag's got 50 stars.
The police make choices that are tough.
But in this case, the people had enough.

Losing your home is a troubling sign.
Let's pretend everything's just fine!

This is getting awfully serious.
Are we sure we're not delirious?

People lost homes they could no longer afford.
Their pleas to keep working, mostly ignored.

Persisting for months, the sickness
raised many concerns.
It refused to be suppressed *(unlike
someone's tax returns).*
Employers had to send workers away,
even some without pay.

Even so, the world changed.
Movies, sports, and vacations, cancelled.
School schedules, rearranged.

Yucky meter

The sickness caused much dread,
but our great leader kept a cool head.
Blabbing to the public is too much
information.

After all,
who needs
education?!

Poor forest management was to blame.

Climate change is a hoax!

We just need some leaf sweepers, folks.

Yucky meter

The first yucky thing was brushfire down under.
Koalas' lives were torn asunder.

The president checked all his "facts" in making this claim:

How could it be THAT bad, you ponder?

Don't let the media make your mind wander!

EVERYBODY HAD A YUCKY TIME

How to explain 2020 to kids (in rhyme)

M.A.G.A. Edition

MAKE AMERICA GREAT AGAIN

Christopher Buttons

ISBN: 978-0-9982197-9-0

Fair
warning:

Hints of
sarcasm
may follow.